A MRS. K. BOOK

Growing up Safe

Safety
winter

Illustrated by Sue Wilkinson

SAFETYVILL

Safetyville Hospital

Safetyville School

Police Station

Badgerson's House

McHare's House

FRED'S Garage

SAFETY SERIES

PUBLISHER	Joseph R. DeVarennes
PUBLICATION DIRECTOR	Kenneth H. Pearson
ADVISORS	Roger Aubin
	Robert Furlonger
EDITORIAL MANAGER	Jocelyn Smyth
EDITORS	Ann Martin
	Robin Rivers
	Mayta Tannenbaum
PRODUCTION MANAGER	Ernest Homewood
PRODUCTION ASSISTANTS	Martine Gingras
	Catherine Gordon
	Kathy Kishimoto
	Peter Thomlison
PUBLICATION ADMINISTRATOR	Anna Good

SPECIAL CONSULTANT	*Barbara Jarvis*
ILLUSTRATION AND DESIGN	Sue Wilkinson

Canadian Cataloguing in Publication Data

Main entry under title:

Safety in winter

(Growing up safe; 14)
ISBN 0-7172-2460-0

1. Winter sports—Safety measures—Juvenile literature.
2. Outdoor recreation—Safety measures—Juvenile literature.
I. Wilkinson, Sue.   II. Series

GV191.625.S33 1988   j796.9'028'9   C88-094238-X

Come join Jessica, Trevor and Lori Bearberry as they find out everything they need to know about winter safety.

DRESS WARMLY FOR THE COLD WEATHER.

STAY WELL BACK FROM PASSING SNOWPLOWS.

DO NOT WALK IN THE PILES OF SNOW LEFT BY THE SNOWPLOW.

DO NOT THROW SNOWBALLS AT PASSING VEHICLES.

BE CAREFUL WHEN PLAYING
WITH SNOWBALLS. ICE OR
STONES INSIDE CAN HURT
OTHERS.

DO NOT RUN ON ICY SIDEWALKS.

DO NOT WEAR LONG SCARVES. THEY COULD GET CAUGHT IN SKATES, SKIS, TOBOGGANS . . .

USE SKATEGUARDS WHEN CARRYING YOUR SKATES.

DO NOT GO ONTO A FROZEN LAKE OR RIVER UNLESS A SAFE SIGN IS POSTED.

SKATE WITH A GROWNUP IN A SUPERVISED AREA.

DO NOT PUSH OTHER SKATERS.

DO NOT TOBOGGAN NEAR A ROAD.

CHECK THAT YOU WON'T HIT ANYONE BEFORE TOBOGANNING DOWN A HILL.

CLIMB UP A HILL OUT OF THE WAY OF PEOPLE GOING DOWN.